Errata Slips

Errata Slips

Poems by

Don Thompson

Cover design by Shay Culligan
Cover image by Shayan Rostami on Unsplash
Author photo by Don Thompson

ISBN: 979-8-90146-722-0

Kelsay Books
502 South 1040 East, A-119
American Fork, Utah 84003
Kelsaybooks.com

Seeing is prayer.

—Kimberly Johnson

Contents

III. The Owl's Last Hour

I.
Corrections to the First Edition of Reality

Vernal

Each leaf an errata slip
tipped in to
the Book of Life,
correcting all the mistakes
winter made us make.

Dust

Dust is a non-count noun,
incalculable particles that add up to one.

Ordinarily it settles around us
slowly, even less hurried than time—

dulls the sheen on waxed furniture,
clouds the open eyes
of those reprobates who die alone.

But now and then, dust raises a wall
no one can see through—

a wall that advances on us
like biblical locusts, a virus, a horde
mounted on insolent ponies.

Contra Naturam

In the last autumn, recalcitrant
season that scoffs at natural law,

leaves will neither fall
nor turn amber or russet,

but remain green—like leather
you'd find molding

in abandoned warehouses
where drifters sit by their rubbish fires

and stare into them
with no thoughts left to think.

Waiting

More than a thousand years after sunrise,
the day might end. Or not.

You'll watch one cloud for centuries
before it crawls out of sight.

Night will last at least a millennium,
a tabula rasa without stars.

Lead-footed in a dream,
it'll take eons to cross a room

to reach someone who'll be gone
when you get there.

Vague

The dim, noncommittal morning
light seems leftover from yesterday.
It'll have to suffice, I guess.

Overhead, thinnest cirrocumulus
unrolls like a bolt of gauze.
Everything on earth's vague . . .

I miss those hard-edged shadows,
precise as silhouettes
cut from black cardstock by an Xacto knife—

shadows so sharp
you could nick a finger on them
and at least know you're alive.

Transparency

After the river slithers and splats
in rage, whitewater
all the way through the canyon,
it rolls over on its back
and calms down.

Quiet waters, a smooth surface
you can see through.
This is the old trick we fall for . . .

Someone wading knee deep
disappears, tripped
by the current and held under
or deceived by a false bottom
anyone would believe in.

Aquifer

Rivers run through caverns beneath us,
actual and not legendary.
But if you were down there, you'd hear
only the footsteps overhead
of those who believe.

The world's not what you think it is.

The water's cold and serious, metallic
and lifeless—no blind albino fish
die and rot in it,
no insects with extra legs
skitter across the limestone walls.

Drill a well and pump it to the surface
and the water changes—
an exile among us that doesn't speak
the language of light
and never gets used to the taste
of our mouths.

Tupman Road Bridge, California Aqueduct

In the high country, creek water
scratches its back on moss,
practicing its flash and filigree
under the tutelage of benign sunlight.

It could take seasons to feel its way
across a meadow, dawdling.

Now some of that same water
flows beneath my feet
at 13K cubic feet per second—
abducted and rushed to the South
where no thirst's ever been quenched.

Retro

The stars are retro tonight,
a dim incandescence
rather than LED needles in your eyes.

If I'm patient, maybe
they'll make it back to medieval
and glow like thousands of candles
illuminating a cathedral.

And not one will get knocked over,
starting the fire
that burns everything down.

Clear

This clear sky's ominous,
a Babylon wall God could write on,
but for now—blank.

Not even a con trail scrawls
its false prophesy.

And soon, wait-and-see clouds
will shrug up from behind the hills
where they're lying low,
like us—just in case.

Granite

This boulder has stood its ground,
passive but firm,
since the troubled earth extruded it
in the late Paleozoic.

Neither exfoliation, psoriatic lichen
nor weathering matters—
not even the fissure that splits it
down the middle . . .

We're obvious, flesh and bone
confronted by Gnostic rock
not about to let us in on
its deep secrets.

Shadowland

After rain, the plowed field's black
as a shadow—of what,

under obstinate clouds
without sunlight to cast it?

Maybe it's the whole cloth
thousands of shadows will be cut from

by unseen angels with scissors,
diligently snipping silhouettes

to have on hand, ready
when the sun finally comes out.

Anticipation

Water holds still in the ditch,
sunlight shattering on it
without a sound.

Tule reeds like massed antennas
listen—and a frog
hidden among them somewhere,
puffing up and unpuffing.

Everything seems to listen.

A dove cleared its throat
only moments ago
as someone always does
just before the music begins.

II.
Rooted and Uprooted

Our Trees

American-born Chinese elm
in our yard—an unpruned tangle
and panicky in the wind.

An oak, huge and indigenous,
rooted in Yokuts acorn culture.
Branches that resist the wind
until they crack.

An upland pine, not quite upright
and obviously discontented down here.
Its slightly brown needles
flail in the wind like leather whips.

An immigrant palm beside it
arrived not long ago on a wind
that ignored all borders.
Short and stout with outsized fronds
and no complaints.

Nocturnal

The plant blossoms only at night
when it does bloom (not often)
and by noon the petals dissolve
in small rains of dust.

Brittle stems that bend
in spite of themselves,
leaves the color of residual ash
mixed with pulverized bone.

The plant looks dead, but it’s not.
Its withered taproot dips
into brackish water six inches below
where it should’ve given up.

Morning Glory

Spring here begins with bitter yellow
mustard smeared on the slopes
and wild grasses that never quite commit
to green—vibrant
but quick to fade in sunlight like cheap paint.

An austere landscape, enhanced
only by hallucinogenic jimson weed
and morning glory
making its comeback beside the road
until the stoners come along.

Autumnal

November leaves keep the secrets
of cold fire: a death cult
robed in the colors of self-immolation.
Only a ritual. Nevertheless,

they crackle in your clenched fist
like flames and once fallen,
rained on, become soggy
ashes that refuse to turn gray.

Fall

Rubble of leaves instead of stones
after the annual Babylon
has fallen.

And we were its elite—
eunuchs and courtesans, satraps
of everything au courant.

Now we're refugees, shuffling
through leaves into winter,
already making plans to rebuild
our future empire.

November

Trees losing their leaves
like words blown from the pages
of an open book . . .

A few more days of wind like this
and the year will be unwritten.

Feldgrau

Post harvest, before a cold snap,
all the walnut trees in the grove
put on a uniform color—
that muted gray of dust
thick on emerald green.

The trees have nothing to do now.

They stand here as always
in strict rank and file like troops
that have surrendered, waiting
for what will happen next—

that long, forced march into winter,
abandoning yellow leaves as they go.

December

A few campesinos, wearing by habit
outsized summer straw hats,
hoe dead grass in the fog.

Obvious make-work in the last days
before winter layoffs.

And the grass burns reluctantly,
as the year itself does,
all smoke and no fire,
but still smoldering long after dark.

Half-a-Hunger Ranch

The old cabins have gone hungry,
famished for human contact—

now that campesinos live in town
like everyone else.

Windows boarded and doors padlocked,
freshly painted a shade of green

offensive to our sensibilities
that keeps the curious away,

who might peek through a crack
to see what loneliness looks like.

Wait

The word from recalcitrant spring is
wait . . . And its colors so far
comprise a narrow spectrum of gray
from cinder block to gun metal.

You have to get close to a tree
to find green—and then
only a few lackluster buds
and one leaf—

withered and dingy, faded
like a twenty-dollar bill
folded up in a wallet all winter
just in case.

Uprooted

Rain for a week, a surfeit
followed by fierce winds
that knocked down those almond trees
too shallow to take it.

Now they lie flat
with most of their roots exposed,
but exuberant with blossoms
for the last time.

Two Trees

Impervious bark, aloof with unyielding
needles three hundred feet up,
sequoias prevail, show-offs
who've achieved the pinnacle
of self-actualization.

You pose next to them
to signal humility . . .

Bristlecone pines play dead
for thousands of years,
self-whittled to a twisted nub
with nothing to boast of
and roots like stone
inseparable from solid rock.

III.
The Owl's Last Hour

Ant Lions

In fields where only burrs took root
that could puncture my Keds,

fierce little predatory larvae
prepared their traps:

funnel-shaped amalgams
of useless loose dirt and sand.

No traction for insects that blundered in
or I sacrificed, watching them

slip struggling down into that hour glass
with no bottom half below its aperture—

only the sickle jaws,
although it never occurred to me,

of time itself.

Local Ornithology

Nowadays we have no colorful birds,
if we ever did,
only an augmented spectrum of browns
from dulce de leche to espresso.

But an oriole shows up every spring
wearing gypsy yellow.
Some hummingbirds shimmer,
slightly, and so do

those raspberry-headed house finches—
as if a fluorescent angel
rubbed them with his thumb
for luck.

Honeydew

Evidence of autumn: bees
up early and hard at work
in the Chinese elm,
even though it's no longer in blossom.

An urgent, electric hum
of gleaners loading up
on aphid excretion from sticky leaves
to make the year's final honey.
Not bad—

if you have a taste for dark
and iffy, last-chance sweetness.

Sonata

The doves' duet for alto flutes,
which must be in D minor,
performed again this evening
reminds me of how much sorrow there is
and how grief accrues to grief
as darkness comes on.

Later, two owls will sing
the second movement—variations
of the same motifs
in a lower, more ominous octave.

The third movement will be Silence.

Shard

Poking around an abandoned homestead,
you might find a shard
among the crumbs of adobe—
not earthenware water pot, but china
glazed an exhausted color
too pale to be white:

Someone’s Sunday-only place settings
that came who knows how far
wrapped in bed linen and under garments
to arrive safely.

Scant portions for years, then none,
and the plates finally shattered
in a rage of failure and isolation . . .

The moon tonight, waning gibbous phase,
is like that shard, lonelier
to look at than anything I’ve ever seen.

Light

In the owl's last hour,
prey becomes prey to early,
not quite illusory light.

Darkness begins to break apart
so that things once more have shadows
with gaps between them

any mouse has to skitter across—
almost safe, almost home.
Owl eyes miss nothing that moves.

Venite Dominum

Darkness is a lantern for mice,
for cautious toads, showing the way
out of the light that exposes them.

Owls are lamps unto themselves,
snipers with night vision goggles.

My owlishness prays to be fed,
beseeches God
for the taste of blood
and for the pulse fading in my grip.

My mouseness prays for mercy,
cowers into solitude, knowing
every dark corner of the mind.

Soliloquy

The night bird's soliloquy falters,
though heartfelt, and stutters into silence.

I'd prompt him with a whisper if possible,
if I knew the avian canon.

At least there's no audience out there,
no crickets chattering in the pit.

One owl up in the balcony boos
on his way out.

Out of the Past

This wind may not blow from the north
but out of the past—
centuries old with its *thee* and *thou*

in an accent no longer understood
that must be the King James version
as originally spoken.

In its blunt lexicon, the wind
utters rebukes
no one takes to heart anymore

and puts curses on us,
almost inexpressible
in our timid circumlocutions.

Vulture

Tattered black habit with a red cowl
to hide blood stains, a monk
ministering to the unburied dead
who offers them, faithfully,
a harsh mercy . . .

Lifts his head now as if listening
to God whisper
something
we're not holy enough to hear.

Sanctified

I think the coyote I saw this morning
had gone hungry on purpose—
fasting not starving.
And not out to hunt
but to take a solemn walk
and meditate.

That's how he looked anyway,
shabby in mendicant fur
with a holy glow . . .

Maybe everything's trying
to get right with God:

Penitent trees shed leaves still green;
stones with their sandals off
set out on a long, motionless pilgrimage.

Egrets

The egrets have pulled themselves up
by the roots
that dangle uselessly now
as they gain altitude.

No longer earthbound,
they could be huge white flowers
that have learned to fly,
petals repurposed as wings.

About the Author

Don Thompson has been writing about the San Joaquin Valley for over fifty years, authoring two dozen or so books and chapbooks, including *Common Places* (Kelsay Books, 2023) and *Outdoor Chamber Music* (Kelsay Books, 2018). *A San Joaquin Almanac* won the Eric Hoffer Award for 2021 in the chapbook category. Wipf and Stock recently published *The Eightieth Year.*

www.ingramcontent.com/pod-product-compliance
Lightning Source LLC
LaVergne TN
LVHW090618110826
845146LV00001B/442

* 9 7 9 8 9 0 1 4 6 7 2 2 0 *